Where the River Runs

Where the River Runs

A Portrait of a Refugee Family

Nancy Price Graff

Photographs
Richard Howard

SCHOLASTIC INC.
New York Toronto London Auckland Sydney

Also by Nancy Price Graff and Richard Howard:

The Strength of the Hills: A Portrait of a Family Farm

The Call of the Running Tide: A Portrait of an Island Family

Acknowledgments

We would like to thank the people who helped to make this book possible, particularly Margaret Van Duyne and Harriet Goldstein of One With One, whose work with immigrants and refugees originally led us to Sohka Prek and her family. Their experience with and interest in the problems faced by refugees and immigrants helped us to understand better the difficulties they face. We would also like to thank Charlotte MacLeay, for her careful reading of the manuscript; Maria Muller, for printing the photographs; Jane and George Metzger, for a bed when it was needed; the teachers and administrators of Thomas Gardiner School for their interest in the book; and Henry Dunow and John Keller, for their support. This book would not have been attempted or finished without the participation and enthusiasm of Frances Srulowitz. We are deeply grateful for all of her help. Finally, we would like to express our warm appreciation to Sohka Prek; to her mother, Sok Eng; and to her sons, Buttra, Oudom, and Richard, who shared their lives and stories with us even when it was painful for them to do so. We felt humbled in the presence of their determination, courage, and integrity.

Text copyright © 1993 by Nancy Price Graff.
Photographs copyright © 1993 by Richard Howard.
All rights reserved. Published by Scholastic Inc., 555 Broadway, New York, NY 10012, by arrangement with Little, Brown and Company Inc., Boston.
Printed in the U.S.A.
ISBN 0-590-20362-2

1 2 3 4 5 6 7 8 9 10   14   01 00 99 98 97 96 95 94

To my husband, Christopher
    — N. P. G.

To John Ramsey and Anna Faith Jones, for all their support
    — R. H.

In the United States, even today, there are pilgrims. At Thanksgiving, as they are seated around the table, they may not look like the pious, black-frocked Puritans who arrived on the *Mayflower* almost four hundred years ago, but they are pilgrims just the same. All of them have come for the same reason that generations of pilgrims came before them: to build a new and better life for themselves.

Each year, almost half a million immigrants and refugees enter the United States. They arrive by boat and plane, by car and on foot. Many come with little more than what they can carry. All of them come because the countries they left could not provide them with good jobs or modern education or homes or food or freedom or sometimes even just with hope.

Immigrants come because they want to. Often they have waited and saved their money for years for the chance to start their lives over again. To them, the United States is a land of vast and exciting opportunities. Refugees come because they have to. Displaced by war or famine or unimaginable poverty or threatened with death for what they think or say or write, they cannot survive in their homelands. They go wherever they can find a country willing to take them in. To refugees who come here, the United States offers not just a chance for a new life but a chance at life itself.

All the pilgrims who come leave behind many things that were important to them, but they also bring something of their homelands with them. In the United States, where almost everyone is an immigrant or a refugee or the descendant of one or the other, many of the ideas and recipes and customs and languages that pilgrims carry in their heads and hearts have taken root like seeds and grown. This explains why Americans celebrate Saint Patrick's Day, why we eat egg rolls and burritos, and why we use words like *rendezvous* and *gesundheit*.

Sohka Prek and her three sons, Buttra (BOO-tra), Oudom (OH-dowm), and Richard, are modern pilgrims. They have come as refugees to the United States because a seventeen-year-old bloody civil war in Cambodia has killed perhaps as many as three million Cambodians and left the country in ruins. They have been here for six years now, and they have been working hard to make a new life for themselves.

Over Thanksgiving dinner at the home of their friend Frances Srulowitz in Cambridge, Massachusetts, near Boston, Buttra, Oudom, and Richard tell their mother about the Pilgrims, whom they have been studying in school. The story they tell is one of courage and pain and extraordinary strength. But the story of people who have been uprooted and driven to new lands is older even than the *Mayflower;* it is as old as humankind. This is the story of a refugee family and of what it is like to be modern pilgrims in a strange new land.

In the morning, when the sky is still gray with the first light of dawn, the birds start singing in the tree outside the bedroom that eight-year-old Oudom shares with his brothers, Buttra and Richard. Cardinals, blue jays, grackles, mourning doves, and even sea gulls flock to the large pine, and together they make such a racket that Oudom has trouble sleeping past this raucous announcement that the day has begun. If he lived in a small, rural village in Cambodia, in an open, airy house on stilts, as most Cambodians do, Oudom's day would begin with similar sounds of the countryside awakening. But this is Allston, Massachusetts, where Oudom lives with his mother and brothers in an apartment surrounded by apartments and houses filled with families from many lands.

Although it is part of Boston, one of the oldest cities in the United States, Allston is a neighborhood of newcomers. Many of its residents are immigrants, people who left the country of their birth by choice to come to the United States and begin their lives anew. Many of Allston's other residents are refugees, people who were taken in by the United States after having been driven from their native lands by fighting, famines, natural disasters, or civil wars. Today the population of Allston includes of people who were born in Cambodia, Laos, Vietnam, China, Brazil, India, the former republics of the Soviet Union, Thailand, Haiti, Pakistan, many different countries in Africa, and at least a half dozen Spanish-speaking countries, such as Mexico and El Salvador. Many came from rural villages, where they often woke to the songs of birds, but all of them now find themselves in a busy, crowded city where the corner stores sell music from Guatemala, pottery from China, and shoes from Brazil. Here the bird songs are a gift of music that does not depend on being able to understand English and a daily reminder of the lives they once lived and left behind.

By the time Oudom opens his eyes, his mother is already up and dressed, ready to leave for her job. Sohka works for the state of Massachusetts, helping families without much money learn about good nutrition and receive the food they need to be healthy. She enters the boys' bedroom and wakes Buttra and Richard, then kisses all her sons good-bye. While parents all over the city coax their children through their morning routines and get them off to school, ten-year-old Buttra does his part in this busy household by taking responsibility for fixing breakfast for himself, Oudom, and six-year-old Rich-

ard. He also makes sure everyone is dressed and washed and that they all get to school on time, with their lunches and homework in hand.

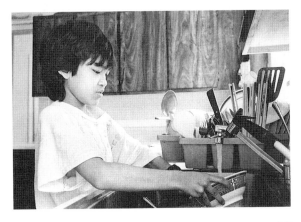

The Thomas Gardner School, just three blocks away, reflects the variety of Allston like a mirror. Its hallways are filled with a

chorus of voices of five hundred children from eighteen different countries. These children have come from places where, for example, everyone uses gourds to drink water drawn by hand from village wells, or where ancient tribal customs encourage men to have many wives in order to have many children, or where it is considered unsanitary to eat with your left hand, or where dog meat and birds' nests are delicacies, or where everyone sits on the floor because there is no such thing as a chair. At the Gardner School,

these children are introduced to drinking from water fountains, to families that have just one mother and father, to using silverware, to eating hamburgers, and to sitting on chairs. In time, they will begin to speak English with their friends and teachers. They will also come to understand and appreciate the habits and customs of children from all over the world. But in the meantime, they have much to learn about living in the United States that they will never find in their schoolbooks.

Many of the children at the school come from homes where only Spanish is spoken and understood. Half of them do not speak English well enough to learn in that language the kinds of things that children are traditionally taught in this country. They will spend three years in bilingual classrooms, where both English and Spanish are spoken. There they will learn the language of their new country while they are learning the literature, science, social studies, and math that children everywhere in the United States are learning in English-speaking schools. After three years, they will move into classrooms where only English is spoken and where the Spanish they learned to speak as babies is now treated like a foreign language.

Because there are fewer of them and because they come from so many different countries, children from non-Spanish-speaking countries, such as Cambodia and Haiti, India and Iran, are not placed in classrooms by themselves at the Gardner School. Instead, they are placed in classrooms

where English is the language of learning. As they take their seats next to children with whom they may have much in common but few ways to share it, they can sense anger and happiness, orders and secrets, jokes and conversation, but the words that convey these feelings and ideas are meaning-

16

less. Until the new children learn to communicate with more than their hands and eyes and smiles, the lack of a common language will be like a stone wall low enough to see over but too high to scale. In time, they will learn how to ask for a piece of paper, to play kickball, to tell the story of George Washington and the cherry tree, and to laugh at knock-knock jokes, but even after they learn enough English to do these things, many of them will continue to speak another language at home with their parents and grandparents and perhaps among their parents' friends. Few of them will forget what it was like at first to be in a classroom where, for awhile, nearly every word spoken — in English and many other languages — was as unfamiliar to their ears as the songs of whales.

In Buttra's, Oudom's, and Richard's classrooms, few of the other children are from Cambodia, but they have no trouble understanding their teachers or their English-speaking classmates. After six years in the United States, all three boys speak English fluently and without a Cambodian accent. They continue to pick up new English words now the way almost every child does, by listening to their friends and to English-speaking adults, by reading books,

and by watching television. They are also learning things that students in schools filled with children who have more similar backgrounds may never know, about holidays in the African nation of Cameroon, for example, and what the Chinese eat for their new year's celebration. These holidays and customs are on the calendar each day at the Gardner School because many of the school's teachers came, as Oudom and Buttra did, from another country. They know from their own experience that people's familiar customs and traditions cannot just be left behind like pieces of outgrown clothing.

At noon, after half a day of kindergarten, of eating Rice Krispies and bagels for breakfast, of practicing the letters of the alphabet, and of speaking English to his teacher and classmates, Richard greets his grandmother in Khmer (Ka-MEER), the ancient language of Cambodia. She has walked to the school from her apartment half a mile away to take him home. Every day, Sok Eng shows again her appreciation for Richard's teacher by folding her hands beneath her chin and bowing slightly. This is *sompeah,* the traditional way Cambodians greet and show their respect for people, such as teachers, whom they consider wise or important. The next instant, she smiles and says to Richard's teacher, "Hi. How you doing?" But Sok Eng knows few English words beyond these. Behind her bright eyes is the constant fear that she will not understand something someone will say to her. She has learned to watch Richard's teacher's face carefully for a reply and gleans as much from that as from any words exchanged about how things have gone at school today for her grandson.

Sok Eng is dressed as she often dresses, in the sarong, or wrapped skirt, that is traditional for Cambodian women. The small steps she takes in the long, tight skirt match Richard's short steps, and they leave together to walk back to Richard's family's apartment. As he steps out through the school's large front door, Richard leaves behind not just his friends but the English language and customs that he shares with them. From noon until mid-afternoon, when his older brothers get home, Richard's world is Cambodian.

Together, he and his grandmother leave their shoes at the door of the apartment, because that is the custom in Cambodian homes. Sok Eng prepares a Cambodian lunch for him of chicken soup or rice and Cambodian egg rolls, called spring rolls. Afterward, they watch Cambodian television on cable, afternoon soap operas that are available to the large Cambodian-speaking

population in and around Boston, and they talk in Khmer, because although Sok Eng speaks three languages and Richard two, Khmer is the only language they have in common.

When Buttra and Oudom arrive home, the transition they make is not nearly as complete as the one Richard makes at noon. Like Richard, they speak Khmer with their grandmother, but all three boys speak English among themselves. The books and homework they bring home are in English as well. The friends they meet in the neighborhood to play with and those in the park, where they go to play kickball and tag in the afternoon, come from many different lands, but the common language is, once again, English. All afternoon and into the evening, the television channels flip between the Cambodian station, whose characters transport Sok Eng's imagination back to the world she left behind when she fled Cambodia, and American stations, where the boys meet Teenage Mutant Ninja Turtles and Mickey Mouse and other symbols of the culture of which they have grown to feel most a part.

For dinner, the boys eat the kind of food their grandmother knew as a child in Cambodia and that she learned to cook as a young bride and mother.

It is nothing like the bread or the spaghetti or the other foods they see and sometimes eat at school, but it is the kind of food they have eaten all their lives, and they love it. Each evening, their grandmother's pots simmer and sizzle with spicy fried rice and rice noodles; warm white rice; spring rolls; *bawbaw,* a chicken soup with Asian vegetables; or any of the other traditional dishes that Sok Eng manages to make using the foods she and Sohka find in the Asian markets of Boston. Everyone eats in the living room, sitting on the couch or floor, as they would in Cambodia, using the silverware they were introduced to here.

Sohka is rarely able to join her sons and mother for dinner. When her workday ends at five, she gets into her car and drives across Boston through the throng of commuter traffic to Bunker Hill Community College. There, four nights a week, she is taking classes to learn English. In the short time while she waits at her desk before class begins, she finishes up her homework and eats an orange. This small piece of fruit and her determination to learn to write and speak English will have to sustain her for the next four hours.

Although it makes for a long day, the boys wait up for their mother. School, night school, homework, jobs, chores, and friends make their lives so busy that the family does not have enough time to spend with each other. When their mother finally gets home, close to nine-thirty, Buttra, Oudom, and Richard are eager to see her and to share the news of their day, in English. Afterward, Sohka and her mother share their news, in Khmer.

As she does every night, Sohka thanks her mother for making it possible for her to work and to go to school. The words are exchanged in what is no more than a passing moment in the day's activities, but they express a profound truth: the lives of all three generations of this family are as intricately connected as the pieces of a fine puzzle. In the daily struggle to make a better

life for themselves in the United States, they are bound together by need and cooperation as much as by love. Sohka is the centerpiece. With every advance that she makes toward better-paying jobs and a college degree, she carries her whole family with her toward a better life, but the steps would be impossible without her mother's daily help and without Buttra's, Oudom's, and Richard's willingness to be responsible for their homework, school activities, and chores around the house.

In a short while, Sok Eng gathers her few things, puts on her shoes, and leaves to walk back to her apartment. Buttra, Oudom, and Richard are ushered into bed. It is the end of another long day, and everyone is tired.

Sohka says that if she had time to think about her life it would exhaust her, but time is a luxury few refugees give themselves. Like Sohka, they have already lost too much of their lives to the wars and famines and other circumstances that drove them here. She cannot reclaim the years of laughter, play, and schooling that she lost as a teenager to the civil war in Cambodia, nor can she give back to Buttra or Oudom the years they spent in Thailand and the Philippines as babies and toddlers in the desperate conditions of refugee camps, but Sohka does not intend to lose a minute of the life remaining to them.

In the stillness that falls over the apartment at the end of the day, Sohka feels most keenly the way her life has changed since she left Cambodia. Each day there, before the war, she had time to visit with friends, to read books, to go out in the evening, to mingle with the crowds at the markets, to linger over meals with her large family. Now she eats alone the dinner her mother has kept warm for her, then tidies the apartment and gets ready for bed. All too soon, the birds will start singing outside Oudom's window again. By that time, Sohka must already be up and dressed and ready for another day.

Richard was born in Boston soon after his parents, brothers, uncle, and grandmother arrived from a refugee camp in the Philippines, where they had spent eight months waiting to be admitted to the United States. His parents, who would soon be divorced, knew little English, but they knew they needed a special name for this new baby in a new land. Sohka considered the Cambodian names she had bestowed on their first two sons: Buttra, which means prince in Khmer, and Oudom, which means governor. Although Sohka had picked each name carefully at the time, hoping, as all Cambodian parents do, that their children would live up to their names, she knew that neither name had any meaning in the language of this new country. Sohka determined to choose a name for the baby that would give him something to live up to here. Finally she settled on Richard, because the United States looked so rich and prosperous to her after the poverty in which she had spent the last decade of her life. Even today, Richard's name is a symbol of the hopes Sohka has for her sons in the United States and a reminder of the power of new words in a new land.

A refugee family driven to a new land stumbles into a new life as confining and isolating as a box. Without a way to communicate with their new neighbors, to learn what jobs might be available, to tell an employer what skills they have, to explain to a doctor that their head hurts, to know which bus will take them to school, or to ask for something as simple as a battery for a flashlight at a hardware store, they are trapped in a life that is unconnected to the life of the new land going on around them. A new friend may be a window that brightens their lives, but language is the only key that will unlock a door of the box and give them an opportunity for a new life.

Buttra, Oudom, and Richard are lucky to have a key. The two older boys began learning English as soon as they arrived in the United States. Organizations that help refugees and immigrants adjust to their new country helped Sohka find an apartment to rent and arranged for the boys to attend a program where they could begin learning English. The English they learned there and later at school, as well as the knowledge they have picked up about the culture and history of the United States, make it possible for them to feel

at home here and to share in the busy life of the big city in which they now live.

Special friendships have also given them keys they might never have discovered on their own. Frances Srulowitz, who once came weekly to help their grandmother learn English but who has long since stopped giving formal English lessons to Sok Eng, has grown so close to the family that the boys regard her as a favorite aunt. Each week, she comes to read to them and to take them to the public library in Cambridge, where they can choose books. Often she takes them on field trips to museums or parks or to visit her parents' farm in Connecticut. On Saturdays throughout the school year, Frances or Sohka takes the boys to science programs at the Boston Museum of Science. Always Frances is there, even if only at the other end of a telephone line, to offer them a steady stream of information about life in the United States, about the city of Boston, about the schools and government, and about almost everything else from sports to art.

Buttra and Oudom are lucky, too, to have the friendship of Spencer Park and Michael Lim, Asian-American students from nearby Harvard College, whom they met two summers ago through the Boston Refugee Youth Enrichment Program. Like many Cambodian families who fled the civil war, Sohka's surviving family is small and mostly female. With their father and uncle rarely available now, Buttra and Oudom have found Spencer and Michael to be as important as big brothers. Although the program ended at the close of summer two years ago, Spencer and Michael continue to take the boys to the aquarium, the movies, to plays and museums. Spencer is even helping Buttra learn Spanish so Buttra can talk to his Spanish-speaking friends at school. Once or twice a week, Michael and Spencer call Buttra and Oudom on the telephone to chat about homework and movies and anything else that is on the boys' minds, including what it is like to be an Asian-American in the United States today. With Spencer and Michael to encourage them and show them the way, Buttra can talk about becoming a writer or Oudom can talk about becoming a doctor, and both of them can talk about

going to college, all dreams that seemed impossible to realize when Buttra and Oudom arrived in the country as toddlers, penniless and homeless.

Wherever the boys go now, they are able to understand what is going on around them and to talk to the people they meet. After six years in this country, Buttra no longer even thinks in Khmer. At night, in his dreams, everyone speaks English. The box in which all the boys first lived now has many doors, and they can open all of them.

It has been harder for Sohka. Among the very few possessions Sohka brought with her to the United States when she emigrated was a Khmer-English dictionary. The cover is torn and tattered now, the pages worn as smooth as a baby's skin, but this dictionary remains one of the most precious things Sohka owns. From this she can learn that ចូលចិត្ត , or *chole chet,* means to like, or as the Khmer understand it, to enter the heart, as well as the meanings of all the other strange words she hears each day and those she needs to translate herself into English in order for others to understand her. If the languages were more similar, it would be easier, but she has had to learn how

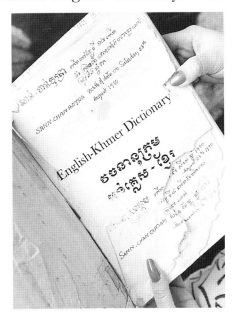

to convert the characters of Khmer Sanskrit to the letters of the English alphabet, how to make sounds that her tongue and mouth were not trained to make when she spoke only Khmer, and how to change the forms of words. In Khmer, for example, there are no plurals or future or past tenses. "I went to the stores yesterday" would be translated into Khmer as "I go to many store yesterday."

For four years, Sohka has been studying in night school the same grammar and vocabulary that her boys are learning by day at school. Even her weekends are full of study. On Saturday mornings, while Buttra stays home and cleans the apartment, Sohka takes Oudom and Richard, the family's dirty clothes, and her homework to the Laundromat. While the younger boys help juggle the washing and drying, their mother conjugates verbs, hoping that one day she will speak English as well as her sons do. She is willing to give so much of her life for her education because learning English is important if she wants to hold better jobs and earn more money. Also, she will need to be fluent in English if she is ever to become a United States citizen and fulfill her dream of going to college and becoming a nurse. But unlike her sons, Sohka will probably never speak without a Cambodian accent, and she will probably never stop thinking and dreaming in Khmer. Her native language is as much a part of her as the light brown of her skin. English will always be a language she acquired and wears on the outside, like the T-shirts and blue jeans that have become a part of her wardrobe in the United States.

Sok Eng, Sohka's mother, has not made even this adjustment and probably never will. Just as she continues to dress often in the colorful sarongs that are the native dress of Cambodia, so she continues to speak the language of her homeland. The reasons Sok Eng has been unable to bring herself to learn English are many and complex. For one, she grew up in a *phum,* or small village, where girls were not educated. She has lived fifty-eight years and learned to speak Khmer, Chinese, and Vietnamese, the languages of her ancestors, without ever having learned to read or write a word in those or any other language. Learning to speak a fourth language now and to read and write for the first time in her life seem too difficult for her and are, in fact, mostly unnecessary within the insulated world of her family where she lives.

She remembers, too, that in Cambodia during the civil war people who could speak, read, or write English were murdered because the new government feared their education. Her dreams of returning one day to Cambodia simply cannot be expressed in a language that she remembers once could have cost her her life. Also, for Sok Eng, the change would be too painful to bear. Replacing Khmer with English in her conversation would be to break finally with the country where her heart still lives. For Sok Eng, the box in which she lives in the United States has no doors that she will ever be able to unlock herself and walk out through alone.

Even the traditional structure of a Cambodian family has been upset by the adjustment to a new language. In Cambodia, children and grandchildren are expected to honor and to pay total obedience to the eldest member of the family. In the United States, however, many of the family conversations in the Prek apartment are no longer held in Khmer. Now the boys almost always talk with their mother in English, and Sok Eng is unable to exert her influence because she can neither express her opinion nor share her wisdom in that language. She is no less honored now within the family than she was when everyone spoke Khmer, but day by day, as her daughter and grandsons speak more English, Sok Eng's place at the head of the family becomes more a symbol of their old life than a position of power and influence in their new one.

These days, Buttra and Oudom must occasionally interpret for their grandmother and guide her through her business in Boston, as if they, and not she, were the head of the family. Even six-year-old Richard sometimes grows impatient with his grandmother's conversations in Khmer. "Grandmother," he says, speaking slowly and clearly, "talk like this: 'I want to go home.'" Sok Eng knows her grandsons love her and are trying in their own way to help her, but it requires grace for her to find herself, the sole remaining elder of her family, sometimes now as helpless as a child in her grandchildren's eyes.

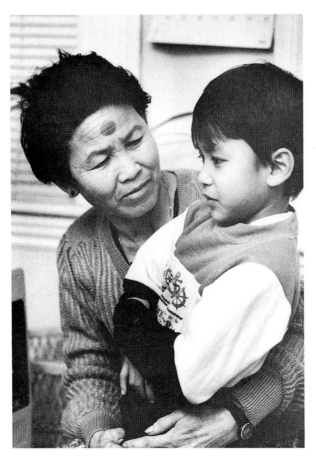

At the Preks' apartment, the kitchen windows are open year-round and a fan often whirs noisily, blowing the fragrant smells of the kitchen out into the air of the city. Inside, despite the ventilation, pale blue smoke and the aromas of shrimp and pork; papaya; lemons; cilantro, or Chinese parsley; and ginger fill the corners of the small room. It is suppertime, and Oudom and Richard are hungry. They mill around underfoot, and finally Sok Eng shoos them out of the room with a wave of her hand and a quick word in Khmer. She is busy right now juggling pots and woks, bamboo steamers and stirring spoons. Still and quiet on a nearby counter is a microwave oven. Next to it is an electric rice cooker, a pot like an oversize Crockpot. It is filled, as it is every day, with warm white rice. Rice is so important to the Cambodian diet that the Khmer vocabulary has words to describe more than one hundred varieties and even a verb, *sii baay,* which means to eat rice. More than anywhere else in the family's life, this room is where their native culture is kept alive and nurtured.

37

Food holds a special place in the lives of refugees and immigrants. This is true not just because they need it to survive and often haven't had enough of it in the past but because the abundance and variety of the foods available in the United States often make it possible for them to reproduce or make the kinds of dishes from their old home that bring them comfort in their new home. Unlike their family possessions, most of which they had to leave behind; their language, which is often of little use here; and their familiar customs, which their new neighbors rarely understand, their recipes travel lightly in their heads and hearts.

Every other weekend, Sohka, Buttra, Oudom, and Richard leave the stores and small shops of Allston, where they do their daily grocery shopping, and drive to Chinatown, in the heart of Boston. For the boys, the chore of shopping is more than compensated for by the opportunity to spend time as a family and by the adventure of visiting Chinatown. Here the streets are narrow and cramped, like most of the streets in the old sections of Boston, but all other similarities end at the curb. The brick buildings here are filled to overflowing with markets, bakeries, and restaurants offering food from China and the countries of Southeast Asia. The sidewalks are crowded shoul-

der to shoulder with many of the more than fifty thousand Laotians, Chinese, Vietnamese, Cambodians, and Koreans who have immigrated to Boston and its suburbs in the past decade.

This busy city with its steel skyscrapers and fast cars could never be confused for the country villages many of these immigrants and refugees left, but this section of Boston comes closest to the bustling markets that were central to the daily life they once knew.

The air is filled with rich, exotic smells and excited chatter in a dozen tongues. Like Sohka and her family, many of these immigrants and refugees come to Chinatown not just for the special foods, which they cannot find in the general supermarkets near their homes, but for the memories the visit conjures up.

Sohka and the boys are shopping today for supplies for a small dinner party that Sohka and her mother will host tonight for friends. Frances comes along, as she often does, to pick up supplies for the Chinese cooking classes she teaches and because outings such as these give her and Sohka and the boys a chance to visit.

The first stop is Hung Cheung Meat Market, Sohka's favorite meat market. The crowd jostles for position in front of a long white counter that is stocked with cuts of fresh meat, most of it pork. The tamarind fruit, lemon grass, and *nam pla,* or fish sauce, that are offered for sale elsewhere in the store cannot be found in traditional grocery stores in the United States, but all of it is in heavy demand here. Sohka quickly finds much of what she needs for tonight's dinner: shrimp, pork, ginger, spring roll skins, bean sprouts, scallions, cilantro, Chinese sausages, and Oriental turnips.

Afterward, they go to See Sun Market, where fifty-pound bags of rice line one wall. The shelves are stocked with specialty foods such as rice-flour cookies, rice-liqueur candy, rice-wine vinegar, spring roll wrappers, and transparent rice noodles spun as delicately as hair. Buttra, Oudom, and Richard help their mother shop, but they also enjoy just browsing along the aisles among the exotic canned fruits and decorated pottery. They rarely ask to buy anything. They know their mother has little money to spare.

Lunch is a treat. Sohka takes her sons and Frances to the Chinatown Eatery, a second-floor food mall, the equivalent of Oriental fast food. Half a

dozen food stalls representing mostly the cuisines of northern and southern China flank a floor crowded with tables and hungry shoppers. Each stall has its own menu and its own specialties. After a brief conference, the group chooses scallion pies from northern China, slivered pig's ears, chow mein with vegetables, fried spiced chicken legs with rice, and slippery, cellophane-like rice noodles. While they wait for the food, Sohka gives Buttra, Oudom, and Richard enough money to play one video game each, and by the time their money is gone, their lunch is ready. Back at the table, each of the boys picks up the chopsticks by his plate as naturally as he would pick up a pencil and begins to talk and eat.

By the time her daughter and grandsons return home in mid-afternoon, Sok Eng is ready to begin cooking. One of her friends has come to help and to visit. On the floor in the middle of the kitchen is a large plastic tablecloth. At the center of the cloth is a clean chopping block, a cleaver, and empty bowls of various sizes. Sok Eng squats on the floor and gets to work, peeling shrimp and turnips, mixing spring roll filling, and dividing and seasoning the chicken. Even with the help of frozen vegetables and Shake 'n Bake seasoning mix, Sok Eng and her friend will need most of the next three hours to prepare the half dozen dishes that are the traditional fare of a special gathering. Sok Eng will spend much of that time squatting on the floor chopping, cutting, and peeling. Although she has cooked in kitchens with counters for six years in the United States, she prefers to cook as she always did in Cambodia where, like most Cambodian women, she squatted on the floor to prepare meals.

Sohka rarely entertains and sees friends only occasionally. Time and money do not allow many extravagances, but sometimes it is necessary for her to put aside both those considerations. The isolation that follows from being a Cambodian refugee in a big American city and the busy pace of life here are two of the hardest aspects of Sohka's new life for her to bear. An occasional dinner party with friends helps ease the loneliness.

Fortunately, Sok Eng loves to cook. She remembers happily the years when she worked in a restaurant in Phnom Penh and still enjoys being asked to cater traditional Cambodian weddings in the area. Tonight she is ready with fried rice, spring rolls, spicy fried chicken, Cambodian beans, and soup redolent with papaya, pumpkin, and eggplant. In the living room, grass mats have been taken from the closet and unrolled on the floor. A plastic tablecloth holds the serving dishes and empty bowls waiting to be filled. When their four friends have all arrived, the women take seats on the grass mats at the edge of the tablecloth and serve themselves from the feast spread out before them. They season the dishes just before they eat them, in the traditional Cambodian way, with sliced scallions, chili sauce, cilantro, lime juice, and bean sprouts. Some of the women eat with chopsticks, some with spoons.

To drink, they choose from steaming Cambodian tea, orange juice, orange soda, and Coke. For two hours the women eat and laugh, filling the air with the excited staccato of Khmer and filling their stomachs with food from home.

For the boys, who straddle the two cultures of their lives more easily than their mother and grandmother do, the Cambodian food they eat at home has been a way for them to learn about a country they have never really had a chance to know. Their grandmother's determination to carry on the cooking traditions of her homeland, despite the way she has been uprooted, is a gift from her to them of a piece of their heritage. Occasionally, they have been able to give her a gift in return.

Buttra introduced his grandmother to pizza, for example. He first tasted it at a friend's house in nearby Chelsea, where he lived with his mother and brothers when they first arrived in the United States. There Buttra met Mark. Mark was a native of Boston, an American child who spoke not a word of Khmer and had never heard of Cambodia. Buttra was a Cambodian child, born in a refugee camp in Thailand, who spoke almost no English, but the two four-year-old boys became fast friends. At Mark's house, Buttra was introduced to pizza. At first, he gagged. The taste and textures were unlike anything he had ever eaten before, but he struggled to swallow it because his friend urged him to and kept telling him how good it was. In time, Buttra acquired the taste. He urged his mother and grandmother and brothers to try it, too, because it was American, and soon they had all come to like it.

Today, although the boys have never learned to like hot dogs or many other American foods, pizza is their favorite food from any culture. Even Sok Eng has learned to say "pizza" and to like it. It is one of the things about her new home that she understands.

The Khmer, the ancient people of Cambodia, believe that life is a river. Sometimes the current is swift, the water treacherous and deep. Then life is hard and difficult to bear. Sometimes the banks are widely set, and the river, clear to the horizon, dances in slow, graceful eddies, a shining symbol of life and hope. Always the future lies downstream, toward the sea, where all rivers empty and where all life begins and ends. Everyone's life follows the river; no one can choose a path different from the channel in which the river runs.

47

In all the dreams Sohka dreamed as a child growing up in Cambodia, she never dreamed that the river would take her to the United States. Immigrants have such dreams. They long to stand on the threshold of a new life that has filled their nights often for years with anxious and exciting visions. But refugees, like Sohka, Sok Eng, Buttra, Oudom, and Richard, never dream of leaving until it becomes impossible to stay. Sohka and her family are in the United States because they were uprooted and driven from their homeland by a bloody civil war. If they wanted to live, they had little choice about leaving and even less choice about where they went. They are here because the river brought them.

Sohka was fourteen in 1975 when the Khmer Rouge, the "Red Khmer" or Communist Khmer, took over Cambodia. The new government emptied the cities and forced everyone into the countryside into collectives, or groups, to plant and harvest rice. Husbands and wives were separated, children were

taken from their parents and from their brothers and sisters. This became known to the Cambodians as *peal chur chat,* the sour and bitter time. Cambodia became a vast prison farm, where everyone worked from before dawn to after dusk. Food was so scarce that people survived by learning to eat snakes, grubs, bugs, and any other food they could scavenge without being caught. In less than a decade, as many as half of the seven million people who once lived in Cambodia died or were murdered by the new government. Sohka's two younger sis-

49

ters died, as did all her uncles and cousins, all but one of her aunts, and most of her friends. Her father disappeared.

Five years later, purely by chance, Sohka found her mother and younger brother in a refugee camp in Thailand. Sohka had grown into a young woman during the years they had been separated, and at first, Sok Eng did not recognize her daughter. With four other teenage girls, Sohka had escaped through the jungles, mountains, land mines, and gunfire of northern Cambodia to Thailand, where thousands of Cambodians were fleeing. There they lived in squalid camps behind tall chain-link fences. All refugees were forbidden by the government of Thailand to leave the grounds and none was able to start life anew, but families were sometimes reunited in the camps, and everyone was safe from the Khmer Rouge and fed regularly for the first time in years. Looking back now at those difficult and frightening years of the *peal chur chat,* Sohka says she does not know why she is lucky enough to be alive.

In the camp, Sok Eng became again the head of a family. Now she was responsible for arranging her daughter's marriage. This is the custom in

Cambodia, where young men and women are not allowed to date each other and where their parents attempt to find a strong, stable family to whom their own family can be bound through marriage. Sohka neither knew nor loved her new husband, but this was less important than the fact that the small, remaining fragment of her family now became part of a large network of people that included not only her husband's family but all the families into which his family had married. Over the next two years, Buttra and Oudom were born in the refugee camp, and some of Sohka's husband's relatives began to emigrate, or leave, for the United States.

The Khmer view of marriage eventually made it possible for Sohka and her family to emigrate. One of her husband's relatives agreed to sponsor them, that is to help them make a new home for themselves in the United States. Soon after, they left for another refugee camp, in the Philippines, and in 1983, when the family finally received permission to emigrate, they were admitted to the United States as "permanent residents" under laws that admit refugees who have no chance of survival in their homeland. Like all immigrants and other refugees, they will have to live in the United States for five years and earn their citizenship by studying American history and learning to read and write in English if they want to be able to vote, to hold public office, to serve on juries, or to enjoy most of the other rights and responsibilities of natural-born citizens of the United States. But in the meantime, they have found an island of safety in the rough water of their life's river.

All the 170,000 Cambodians who have fled that country's civil war and emigrated to the United States bear scars, some inside and some outside. Sohka has two visible ones from a day she discovered a large blood-sucking leech clinging to her left arm while she was on a work crew cutting bananas for the Khmer Rouge. Without thinking, she raised the knife she held in her other hand and frantically used the sharp blade to scrape the leech off. Both the leech and the knife blade left their mark. Sok Eng, like many of the older Cambodian women now in this country, suffers from blinding headaches from the stress of what she has been through. Although western doctors and medicine are now available to her, she prefers to treat her headaches the traditional Cambodian way by lying down and placing a burning candle on her forehead. As the candle burns, Sok Eng believes the flame pulls the negative spirits from her head. She treats her arthritis with similar traditional medicine, by rubbing the edge of a coin the length of her arm. Buttra, his mother and grandmother, and many of the other Cambodian refugees in this country have terrifying nightmares about the "sour and bitter time" and the years they spent in refugee camps. By day, they carry with them everywhere a burden of sorrow. It is like a heavy suitcase they would like to put down but cannot, full of anger and tears shed over the loss of their families and the destruction of their country.

In many ways, life here in the United States has brought them new pains. In her office every day, among the Asian families she translates for and helps, Sohka discovers people like herself who have been cut adrift from their past. They, too, have arrived in the United States without family, family photographs, family heirlooms, usable language, jobs, skills, or sometimes even their family names. Sohka is reminded of this every time she writes her own last name, which was accidentally changed on her immigration forms. At the time, she did not ask to have the mistake corrected because she was afraid that mentioning it would delay her entry or separate her from her family. Instead, she simply gave up her family name. It is one more link broken with her past.

The boys have learned that prejudice is as painful as any wound that bleeds. In stores and malls and other public places, they have been taunted

and looked at suspiciously just because they have cocoa-colored skin and almond-shaped eyes. Even at school, where so many different cultures come together, Oudom says children sometimes slur the word *Cambodian* in unpleasant ways that hurt him and remind him how far his family has had to travel from their homeland. The boys have learned, too, that many people in the United States do not understand the differences that divide the countries of Southeast Asia. Most Americans are unaware, for example, that Vietnamese culture has its roots in China but that Cambodian culture has its roots in India, and that for centuries there have been wars and tensions between these two neighboring countries. In the United States, where Asians from many countries often find themselves living in clusters on the edges of large cities, these deep-seated feelings are not easily forgotten. Nor do many Americans realize that not all Asians are excellent students. Many refugee children, particularly those from Laos and Cambodia, have come not from cities with good schools but from farming villages in the countryside, where book learning was thought to have little value. When Buttra tells the story of being followed once by boys in a car who shouted at him to "Go home!" he shakes his head in hurt and confusion. The United States is the only home he and his brothers have ever really had.

Immigrants and refugees also find sometimes that their own prejudices and stereotypes make it more difficult to adjust to life in a new country. In the culture of Cambodia, for example, light skin is a symbol of status and deserving of *sompeah,* or deference. Cambodians trying to make their way in the United States are often ashamed to admit to a light-skinned person or "white nose" that they do not understand a conversation because to do so would cause them to lose face, or self-respect. In their culture, it would also be the same as accusing the "white nose" of not speaking his own language well enough to make himself understood. This expression of rudeness would violate one of the most important principles of Asian culture, namely that a person must always be self-controlled and polite in public.

In many immigrant and refugee families, the stress of making a new life in a new country pulls the members of a family apart just at the moment when

they need each other most. Sok Eng, Sohka, Buttra, Oudom, and Richard are all traveling at different speeds into their new lives. In many ways, Sok Eng is barely moving at all. She speaks little English, has only Cambodian friends, eats the foods and celebrates the holidays of her ancestors, and spends her days doing the traditional work of Cambodian grandmothers, watching her grandchildren. Sohka is moving much faster. Her English is improving daily, she is educated and employed, her friends are both Cambodians and Americans of other races, she drives, and she is beginning to learn to cook food that is not Cambodian. To their grandmother and mother, the boys are traveling by in a blur. Outside their apartment, they could be American children from anywhere in the country.

Love and need hold them all together, but those ties are strengthened these days by a shared budding interest in Cambodia. Buttra and Oudom are old enough now to be curious about the country their mother and grandmother left behind. On the walls of their apartment are maps of Cambodia so everyone in the family will remember or learn the names of its cities and towns, the places their people came from. Sometimes Sok Eng tells the boys stories about the good days in Cambodia, the days before the Khmer Rouge. Both of the older boys would like to learn to read and write Khmer, and Sohka has promised to teach them. The interest they show in Cambodia and their mother's and grandmother's willingness to help them understand the

life of their ancestors prevent them from traveling like meteors in a straight line away from a Cambodian life and toward an American life. Instead, they are traveling in widening circles like planets in orbit around the life their mother and grandmother once knew.

In early April in Boston, when the maple trees are filled with tight red buds and the daffodils are blooming, Sok Eng begins to think about their garden. It is only a small plot set aside in the small yard that surrounds their apartment building, but the tradition of working in the soil in the spring is an ancient and honored one for all Cambodians who remember how closely their ancestors lived to the land. Buttra, Oudom, Richard, and their grandmother will do most of the planting of carrots and onions and Thai basil. The boys will tend the garden throughout the coming months, and Sok Eng will carry buckets of water to the plants every day if the rains do not come regularly. This is the soul of the life they left behind, and they have found a way even in the city to carry it with them.

Half a world away, the Khmer people are beginning to decorate their Buddhist *wats*, or monasteries, and to prepare the feasts that will accompany their celebration of the Cambodian new year. This national holiday in honor of the start of a new growing season will cover three days filled with worship, food, colorful parades around the *wat*, and the company of friends and family. Schools and offices will be closed. In a country where nearly everyone practices Buddhism, a religion that came to Cambodia from India nearly two thousand years ago, this holiday, or *bonn*, to honor the earth's rebirth, is the most important event of the year.

In Boston, the Cambodian refugees who are making a new life for themselves here will try as best as they can to carry on the traditions of their ancestors. Of course, the schools and offices of Boston will not close to allow them the traditional three days to celebrate, so they will have to squeeze their holiday into a two-day weekend. Neither are there *wats* at which to gather and pray, although there is a temple near Lowell, twenty miles away, to which many Cambodians will travel. The Buddhist monks in their saffron-colored robes will be unable to wander the streets, as they do in Cambodia, with alms bowls outstretched to receive offerings of rice, because the Cambodian community scattered in and around Boston is more an association of the heart than a real village or even a neighborhood.

Instead, Sohka, Sok Eng, Oudom, and Richard gather on Saturday morning with several hundred other Cambodians in the cafeteria of nearby Revere High School. The front of the cafeteria has been transformed with tables into an altar on which the monks sit cross-legged and serene amid all the noise and confusion before the ceremony begins. Around them on the tables is a smorgasbord of food that has been brought for them to eat and bless. Piled on the floor before them are gifts from the families who have come to worship. These offerings of incense, rice, fresh fruit, bouquets of fresh flowers, cans of delicacies, bottles of soda, and money are given in their honor and in memory of dead ancestors. Half of the cafeteria's large floor has been covered with grass mats brought from home. Families squat on these, surrounded by towers of silver carryalls filled with food they have brought

60

to have blessed and to share. All of the women are dressed in brightly colored sarongs that would never have been allowed when the Khmer Rouge made everyone wear black. The subtle fragrance of burning incense fills the room.

Buddhist monks eat just twice a day, at six and eleven in the morning. The ceremony begins shortly before eleven, when the monks start chanting, in English, a prayer that begins, "The suffering of Cambodia has been deep. From this suffering comes great compassion." When they are done with their prayers, offered in both formal Khmer and English, the monks will eat, choosing bites from the many dishes piled around them. Meanwhile, Sohka and her family and everyone around them continues to chant the ancient prayers of Cambodia. Their voices rise and fall like small, quiet waves. Later, when the monks have finished eating, the congregation will have its turn to eat while the monks pray in voices that have the soft, soothing twang of plucked rubber bands.

This is an opportunity that comes rarely in a Cambodian refugee's life. Sok Eng glows with friendship, the comfort of a language and rituals she has known for more than fifty years, and the responsibility, as an elder, for taking

62

63

the collection. Sohka chatters and laughs with friends she otherwise has little time or chance to see. Richard and Oudom sample the foods being passed around and play with other children, all of whom share the heritage of their homeland and an appreciation of what it is like to be a Cambodian child in the United States.

The ceremonies honoring the year of the goat will go on for two days. The hours will be filled with friendship, prayer, and feasting. The Prek family will not stay throughout the ceremony, but Sohka and the boys do return Saturday evening to watch traditional dancing. The dance is sponsored by the Cambodian Community of Massachusetts to raise money for refugee programs. Under the Khmer Rouge, almost all of Cambodia's classical dancers were killed because they represented royalty. In the suburbs of Boston today, the dances are being revived, taught to Cambodian teenagers by refugees who recall the ancient stories they portray and the intricate movements, as fluid and graceful as running water.

To Buttra, Oudom, and Richard, the dances speak of myths and places less clear in their minds than the stories of Paul Bunyan and the streets of Boston, but this is why their mother has brought them. While the boys watch, Richard drinks a Coke, Oudom eats M&M's, and Buttra eats a *pong tea kon,* an incubated duck egg that is boiled and then eaten with pepper, salt, lime, and mint. In Cambodia, this Khmer delicacy is supposed to bring strength and strong blood to those who eat it. In Boston, Buttra eats it because he likes it. As they sit casually in their western clothes, eating foods from two cultures and watching the dancing, the boys show how comfortable they have become in stepping back and forth between the Cambodian culture of their past and the American culture of their future.

This year on Sunday, the second and last day of the Cambodian new year celebration, the Prek family does not retrace their footsteps to the high school. Instead, because the new year coincides with the anniversary of her great-grandfather's death, Sohka hosts a special day-long ceremony honoring her ancestors, particularly her mother. Buttra's bed becomes the altar upon which the monks take their seats. Sohka's coffee table receives the offerings of food and gifts that her friends have brought to be blessed and to share. Friends, young and old, crowd into the rooms onto grass mats that cover the floor. Buttra, Oudom, and Richard keep busy taking coats, answering the door, and playing with friends. In the kitchen, where Sok Eng has been cooking since dawn, her friends flutter around, as excited as young birds. Just before the prayers begin at eleven, the women come in from the kitchen and find seats on the mats before the monks. When they kneel and bow their heads, they fold themselves up like flower buds.

Sohka has all day to express her thanks for her mother, to think, and to pray. In a life that is so busy that Sohka calls it "crazy," this chance to be

66

quiet and thoughtful is rare and welcome. She uses it to pray for all of the members of her family and to think about their future. She hopes her mother will one day feel happy and whole again, either here or in Cambodia if the civil war ends and she is able to return. For herself, Sohka would like the chance to visit Cambodia again and to take Buttra, Oudom, and Richard with her, but she has no wish to return there to live. Cambodia may always be "my country" to her, but Sohka sees the river of her life flowing to the sea as part of the current of life in the United States. The boys already think of themselves as Americans. Their mother hopes they will get a good education because she knows that education is like a ticket for a ride that will take them into the mainstream of the river. But she also hopes they will hold on to some of their Cambodian traditions, such as listening to their elders and supporting her when she gets old.

Mostly Sohka prays for courage and strength for all of them. These are the qualities that brought them here and that have sustained them while they started their lives again. She asks also for opportunity and a sense of belonging. In Khmer or English or any other language, these are the prayers of all pilgrims.

Here is a sampling of questions immigrants and refugees must be able to answer before they can become citizens of the United States.

1. What do the stripes on the flag mean?
2. Who elects the president of the United States?
3. How many changes or amendments are there to the Constitution?
4. How many branches are there in our government?
5. What are the three branches of our government?
6. Who makes the laws in the United States?
7. What is Congress?
8. How many senators are there in Congress?
9. For how long do we elect each senator?
10. How many representatives are there in Congress?
11. For how long do we elect each representative?
12. What is the supreme law of the land?
13. What is the Bill of Rights?
14. Can you name the thirteen original states?
15. Who said, "Give me liberty or give me death"?
16. Who selects the Supreme Court justices?
17. How many Supreme Court justices are there?
18. What is the head executive of a state government called?
19. Who was the main writer of the Declaration of Independence?
20. When was the Declaration of Independence adopted?
21. What is the basic belief expressed in the Declaration of Independence?
22. Where does freedom of speech come from?
23. What is the highest court in the United States?
24. Who was president during the Civil War?
25. Which president is called the "Father of our Country"?
26. Name three rights or freedoms guaranteed by the Bill of Rights.
27. Who has the power to declare war?
28. What kind of government does the United States have?
29. In what year was the Constitution written?
30. Whose rights are guaranteed by the Constitution and the Bill of Rights?
31. What is the introduction to the Constitution called?
32. Name one right guaranteed by the first amendment.

Answers:

1. They represent the original thirteen states.
2. The electoral college
3. Twenty-six
4. Three
5. Legislative, executive, and judiciary
6. Congress
7. The Senate and the House of Representatives
8. One hundred
9. Six years
10. 435
11. Two years
12. The Constitution
13. The first ten amendments to the Constitution
14. Connecticut, New Hampshire, New York, New Jersey, Massachusetts, Pennsylvania, Delaware, Virginia, North Carolina, South Carolina, Georgia, Rhode Island, and Maryland
15. Patrick Henry
16. They are appointed by the president
17. Nine
18. The governor
19. Thomas Jefferson
20. July 4, 1776
21. That all men are created equal
22. The Bill of Rights
23. The Supreme Court
24. Abraham Lincoln
25. George Washington
26. Freedom of speech, press, religion, and peaceable assembly. The right to request change of the government. The right to bear arms. The government may not house soldiers in people's homes during peacetime without the people's consent. A person may not be tried twice for the same offense and does not have to testify against himself. A person charged with a crime still has rights, such as the right to a speedy trial, the right to trial by jury in most cases, protection against excessive or unreasonable fines and against cruel and unusual punishment. The people have rights other than those mentioned in the Constitution. Any power not given to the federal government by the Constitution is a power of either the state or the people.
27. The Congress
28. It is a republic.
29. 1787
30. The rights of both citizens and noncitizens living in the United States
31. The Preamble
32. Freedom of speech, press, religion, and peaceable assembly and the right to request change of the government

71